Elvira Carney
July 02

Baking Bread

D1367011

Making bread –

is traditional cooking at its best. It evokes
memories of old-fashioned bakeries, muscular
kneading and huge, red-hot ovens. Today,
the process is much easier than it was then, but
there is still nothing to compare with the wonderful
smell of freshly baked bread. Best of all, there
are now many more recipes for new kinds of bread.
So let home-baked bread become your own
culinary speciality.

Colour photographs are by
Odette Teubner and Dorothee Gödert

AURA

CONTENTS

A–Z of Baking Bread   4

Rolls and Flat Breads   8

Seed rolls   8
Crusty rolls   8
Pitta bread   10
Flat rye buns   10
Spelt crispbread   12
Sweet wheatgerm crispbread   13
Soya rolls   14
Oat bran rolls   14
Focaccia   16
Bavarian beer breadsticks   18
Grissini   18
Curd cheese rolls   20
Muffins   20

White Bread   22

Classic white loaf   22
Tuscan white bread   24
Baguette   24
Spelt toasting loaf   24
Crispy toast bread   27
Golden toast loaf   28
Rye toast bread   28

Brown Bread   30

Farmhouse bread   30
Swiss country bread   30
Bavarian sourdough bread   32
Double-baked bread   34
Six-grain bread   36
Sunflower seed bread   38
Linseed bread   38
Spelt bread   40
Graham bread   42
Army bread   44
Mixed rye bread   44
Traditional rye bread   46
Corn bread   48
Buckwheat bread   49

Speciality Breads   **50**

Poppy seed loaf   50
Spicy white bread   50
Camembert bread   52
Emmental cake bread   54
Onion bread   56
Savoury bread   56
Aztec bread   58
Walnut bread   60

Index   **62**

Important note   **64**

Baking bread

Baking bread is much easier than many people think and the time and effort involved can be reduced simply by using an electric mixer or a food processor, fitted with dough hooks, for kneading the dough. Breads made with yeast and some other raising agents do need to be set aside to increase in bulk, but you can do something else meanwhile. Just cover the dough with a damp tea towel and leave it in a warm place to rise. The time required varies, depending on the quantity of dough, the temperature, the humidity and a number of other factors. Approximate times are given in all the recipes.

Baking tins

It is not necessary to buy lots of new equipment for baking bread. The ordinary baking trays and tins found in most kitchens are perfectly adequate. Any containers that absorb heat well, such as black loaf tins and cast iron baking trays, are ideal and if you are going to buy new equipment, it is worth bearing this in mind. Loaf tins are designed specifically for baking bread and are usually deeper and wider than cake tins. They are available for baking both 1 kg/2^{1}/$_4$ lb and 500 g/1 ^{1}/$_4$ lb loaves. It is sensible to use the correct size tin for the quantity of dough, as plain yeast breads without extra ingredients will crumble easily if they are baked in a tin that is too large. A small tin gives more crust and a more stable crumb – the soft inner part of the loaf. Breads that need to be baked for a longer time at a lower temperature always require proper metal or ceramic loaf tins. For making toast bread, in particular, it may be worth buying an ovenproof glass loaf 'tin'.

The oven

All standard, conventional ovens, whether powered by electricity or gas, are suitable for baking bread. As a general rule, pale-coloured breads bake best at high temperatures, while dark loaves, such as rye bread, are better suited to a

You can use special loaf tins or ordinary cake tins for baking bread.

ower heat. Some breads, such as toast bread, bake best in the circulating air of a fan-assisted oven, but can still be baked perfectly satisfactorily in a conventional oven. The recipes for breads that are best cooked in this way always include the temperature for a fan-assisted oven as well as a conventional one. Microwave ovens are unsuitable for bread-making.

Baking temperatures and times

Modern ovens reach the required temperature within 10–15 minutes. Therefore, you can be 'green' and economical with the preheating time. Preheating time is included in the total preparation time given in all the recipes.

Steam

Many bakers recommend placing a bowl of hot water on the floor of the oven when baking bread. An even better technique may be to dampen the floor of the oven and the walls or the inside of the door when preheating or before putting in the loaf. This ensures a steamy atmosphere as soon as the oven is hot and is especially suitable for breads made from yeast dough. The steam helps the dough to rise, giving the loaf a good shape and a light crumb. During the second half of the baking time, the loaf requires dry heat.

Always follow the oven manufacturer's instructions when dampening the oven and do not put water for steaming into it when it is switched on.

Trouble-shooting

There are several, easily avoided, common mistakes when making bread.

1. The dough is too stiff and dry, the bread acquires a very pale, hard crust and is edible only on the day it has been baked. To avoid this, make sure that the dough and the top surface of the loaf are damp enough to ensure that the crust becomes dry and crisp.

2. The loaf overflows the sides of the tin. This is the result of not allowing the dough sufficient time to rise before the loaf is put in the oven. It is essential to set aside the dough long enough for it to rise until its bulk has increased by one-third. Suggested rising times in the recipes are guidelines only.

3. The loaf is 'heavy' and has a greasy crumb. This happens when the dough is too wet or did not visibly ferment after each rising. Use less liquid or extend the rising time (for example, if you are using old yeast). Only continue the next stage of kneading or baking if the bulk of the dough has clearly increased.

4. The dough does not rise. This may happen if the ingredients were too cold. Before using flour, leave it in a warm place for a few hours. Alternatively, the liquid added to the yeast may have been too hot and, therefore, killed it. It should never be hotter than lukewarm, that is, hand-hot.

Liquid

The classic liquid used for making bread is water. Milk, buttermilk and yogurt are also used and each has its own particular effect. Curd cheese is excellent for many kinds of dough. The quantity of liquid required depends on the water-, protein- and bran-content of the flour, all of which may vary according to where it was grown and from year to year. Most types of dough should be fairly wet – even so wet that they are unpleasant to knead by hand and are better kneaded in a food processor.

Yeast

There are several different kinds of yeast. Fresh yeast is available in 40 g/1 1/2 oz cubes from health-food shops and supermarkets. Store it in the refrigerator. It is more economical than dried yeast.

Dried yeast can be kept longer than fresh and is a useful store-cupboard item for spontaneous bakers. You can, of course, use dried yeast in all the recipes in this book and 15 ml/1 tablespoon dried yeast is the equivalent of 15 g/1/2 oz fresh. Use it in the same way as fresh, but if the dough is very stiff, you can add 15–30 ml/1–2 tablespoons water.

Easy-blend dried yeast, sometimes called fast-action yeast, is very convenient as there is no need to mix it with the liquid first. It can be combined directly with the dry ingredients and then the warm liquid can be added.

The most important flours at a glance: 1 plain white flour 2 wholemeal flour 3 soya flour 4 unbleached flour 5 stoneground flour 6 buckwheat flour 7 rye flour

All kinds of yeast have a use-by date stamped on them. You can sometimes still use the yeast when the date has only just passed, but this is not recommended. Never use fresh yeast that has gone hard or smells disgusting. If you are using old yeast, you will have to lengthen the rising times. If you are in doubt about fresh or ordinary dried yeast, set the mixture aside in a warm place for 10 minutes. If it is not foamy, throw it away.

Equipment

An electric mixer fitted with one or two dough hooks makes kneading easy. If you want to bake a lot of bread frequently without 'getting your hands dirty', then it is worth buying a large capacity food processor with a powerful motor and a strong kneading attachment.

Flour

Nowadays, there is a wider choice of household flours available from supermarkets, making it possible to bake many different types of bread. Most recipes in this book use the kinds of flour that are available in supermarkets and health-food shops. Strong white flour or bread flour is the most popular choice. Milled from hard or durum wheat, it has a high gluten content. It produces an elastic dough that makes it especially suitable for yeast cookery. Plain white flour is a useful, all-purpose flour that may be used on its own or in combination with other flours for some types of bread, although it is more commonly used for cakes and pastries. Stoneground flour, as might be expected from its name, is wheat flour ground in the traditional way between two stones rather than milled. It has a better flavour than milled flour, but does not keep well. Wholemeal flour is wheat flour milled from the whole grain, with nothing added or removed, and, for many people, is the healthy option.

A more unusual flour is spelt, an ancient variety of wheat. It is still popular in some parts of northern Europe and can be obtained from some health-food shops. It is a relatively soft grain and the flour is often combined with rye flour for bread-making. Rye flour is darker than wheat flour but is its nutritional equal. It contains less gluten, so it makes a slightly less elastic dough. It is quite often combined with wheat flour for making bread. Other cereals, such as cornmeal and soya flour, are used for making speciality breads.

Always store flour in a cool, dry place. Most types will not keep very long and should always be discarded when the use-by date has passed.

Salt
Commercial bakers tend to be lavish with salt, which is contrary to current nutritional guidelines. Salt serves to pre-serve and stabilize and adding a moderate quantity will not be harmful. You can use as much or as little salt as you like or need in home-made bread. However, using very little salt alters the crumb (the soft inner part of the loaf), so that it usually has bigger air holes, as, for example, Tuscan white bread (see page 24). A loaf will not keep quite so well if you use only a little salt, but then, one of the joys of home-made bread is to eat it still warm from the oven, so the question of storage does not arise. If you do want to keep a lightly salted loaf, freezing is the best way.

Sourdough
This is a raising agent made from rye or wholemeal flour, water and a 'starter', such as honey or buttermilk. It is made several days ahead of baking – usually at least five – and must be stored in an earthenware, ceramic or glass container at room temperature. It is ready when the mixture is frothy and has a strong, sour smell.

Water
You need water to dampen the oven and to sprinkle on the freshly baked loaf. The best way is to use a mister kept for the purpose. Fill it freshly each time and, after use, empty it, leave it to dry thoroughly and store the top and base separately. Water can also be brushed on the loaf with a large pastry brush. Brushing or spraying the hot loaf with water produces a beautiful golden colour and makes it crisp and easy to cut.

Other ingredients
Sugar, honey and treacle help speed up fermentation. Treacle colours rye bread and makes it aromatic. Butter, vegetable oil and lard make many kinds of dough softer and crumblier and add to the bread's toasting qualities. Many spices and seeds, such as caraway and coriander, add flavour and make bread more digestible.

A houseplant mister spray and a wide pastry brush are useful and inexpensive pieces of equipment when baking bread.

Seed rolls

Economical

Makes 12 rolls
400 g/14 oz strong white flour
40 g/1 1/2 oz fresh yeast
10 ml/2 teaspoons sugar
250 ml/8 fl oz lukewarm water
15 ml/1 tablespoon vegetable oil
5 ml/1 teaspoon salt
butter, for greasing
5 ml/1 teaspoon poppy seeds
5 ml/1 teaspoon sesame seeds
5 ml/1 teaspoon caraway seeds
5 ml/1 teaspoon linseed

Approximately per roll:
560 kj/130 kcal
4 g protein
2 g fat
25 g carbohydrate

● Approximate preparation
time: 1 hour 50 minutes,
including rising and cooking

---

1. Sift the flour into a large bowl and make a well in the centre. Crumble the yeast into the well and sprinkle the sugar over it. Pour in the water and mix the yeast, sugar and a little of the flour into a thin paste. Cover and set aside in a warm place for about 15 minutes.

2. Gradually knead in the rest of the flour, the oil and salt. Form the dough into a ball, cover and set aside for about 15 minutes. Grease a baking sheet.

3. Knead the dough until smooth and elastic, then divide it into 12 equal pieces. With damp hands, shape each piece into a ball. Place the balls on the baking sheet and flatten them slightly. Brush with

water, Mix the all the seeds together in a small bowl and sprinkle them on the rolls, pressing them in. Cover and set aside in a warm place for about 10 minutes, until the bulk of the dough has increased by about one-third.

4. Meanwhile, spray the floor and sides of the cold oven with water. Preheat it to 240°C/475°F/Gas 9. Bake the rolls for 30–35 minutes, until they are golden brown. Turn off the oven, but leave the rolls in it for a further 5 minutes.

5. Transfer the rolls to a wire rack and spray or brush cold water all over them.

Crusty rolls

Exquisite

Makes 12 rolls
400 g/14 oz strong white flour
40 g/1 1/2 oz fresh yeast
10 ml/2 teaspoons sugar
250 ml/8 fl oz lukewarm water
15 g/1/2 oz lard
5 ml/1 teaspoon salt
butter, for greasing
15–30 ml/1–2 tablespoons
   clear honey
15–30 ml/1–2 tablespoons white
   wine vinegar
15 ml/1 tablespoon sea salt

Approximately per portion:
590 kj/140 kcal
4 g protein
2 g fat
26 g carbohydrate

● Approximate preparation
time: 1 hour 40 minutes,
including rising and cooking

---

1. Sift the flour into a large bowl and make a well in the centre. Crumble the yeast into the well and sprinkle the sugar over it. Pour in the water and mix the yeast, sugar and a little of the flour into a thin paste. Cover and set aside in a warm place for about 15 minutes.

2. Gradually knead in the rest of the flour, the lard and salt. Form the dough into a ball, cover and set aside for about 15 minutes. Grease a baking sheet.

3. Knead the dough until smooth and elastic. Divide it into 12 equal pieces. Shape each piece into a ball and place on the baking sheet. To make pretzels roll each piece into 1 cm/1/2 inch thick sausages. Tie into a loose knot.

4. Mix 15 ml/1 tablespoon each honey and vinegar to a smooth paste for round rolls or 30 ml/ 2 tablespoons each for pretzels. Brush the rolls with the paste and sprinkle with the salt. Cover and set aside in a warm place for about 10 minutes, until the bulk of the dough has increased by one-third.

5. Meanwhile, spray the floor and sides of the oven with water. Preheat it to 240°C/475°F/Gas 9. Bake the rolls for 30–35 minutes, until they are golden brown. Turn off the oven, but leave the rolls in it for a further 5 minutes.

6. Transfer the rolls to a wire cooling rack and spray or brush cold water all over them.

Above: Crusty rolls
Below: Seed rolls

Pitta bread

Easy

Makes 6 pittas
400 g/14 oz plain white flour,
* plus extra for dusting*
40 g/1 1/2 oz fresh yeast
15 ml/1 tablespoon honey
250 ml/8 fl oz lukewarm water
120 ml/4 fl oz olive oil
10 ml/2 teaspoons sea salt
butter, for greasing
10 ml/2 teaspoons sesame seeds
1 teaspoon black mustard seeds or
* cumin seeds (optional)*

Approximately per portion:
1,600 kj/380 kcal
8 g protein
17 g fat
51 g carbohydrate

- Approximate preparation
  time: 2 hours, including
  rising and cooking

---

1. Sift the flour in a large bowl and make a well in the centre. Crumble the yeast into the well and add the honey. Pour in the water and mix the yeast, honey and some of the flour to a thin paste. Cover and set aside in a warm place for about 15 minutes.

2. Gradually knead in the rest of the flour, the oil and salt. Form the dough into a ball, cover and set aside for about 15 minutes.

3. Grease a baking sheet. Knead the dough until smooth. Divide it into 6 equal pieces and roll them in flour. Slap each piece of dough between floured palms to make a 15 cm/6 inches round. Place on the baking sheet, brush lightly with water and sprinkle with the seeds, pressing them in. Cover and set aside in a warm place for about 15 minutes, until the bulk of the dough has increased by one-third.

4. Meanwhile, spray the floor and sides of the oven with water. Preheat it to 240°C/475°F/Gas 9.

5. Prick holes in the pittas with a skewer. Bake for 25–30 minutes. Switch off the oven, but leave the pittas in it for a further 5 minutes. Transfer to a wire rack to cool.

Flat rye buns

Easy

Makes 6 buns
200 g/7 oz plain white flour
200 g/7 oz rye flour, plus extra
* for dusting*
40 g/1 1/2 oz fresh yeast
15 ml/1 tablespoon black treacle
300 ml/1/2 pint lukewarm water
5 ml/1 teaspoon caraway seeds
2.5 ml/1/2 teaspoon fennel seeds
2.5 ml/1/2 teaspoon anise
10 ml/2 teaspoons sea salt
butter, for greasing

Approximately per portion:
960 kj/230 kcal
7 g protein
1 g fat
50 g carbohydrate

- Approximate preparation
  time: 1 3/4 hours, including
  30 minutes rising time and
  40 minutes cooking time

---

1. Sift both types of flour into a large bowl and make a well in the centre. Crumble the yeast into the well and add the treacle. Pour in the water and mix the yeast, treacle and some of the flour to a thin paste. Cover and set aside in a warm place for about 15 minutes.

2. Gradually knead in the rest of the flour, the caraway seeds, fennel seeds, anise and salt. Form the dough into a ball, cover and set aside for about 15 minutes. Grease a baking sheet.

3. Knead the dough until smooth and elastic. Divide it into 6 equal pieces and roll them in rye flour. Slap each piece of dough between floured palms to make a 15 cm/6 inches round. Place the buns on the baking sheet. Cover and set aside in a warm place for about 15 minutes, until the bulk of the dough has increased by one-third.

4. Meanwhile, spray the floor and sides of the oven with water. Preheat it to 240°C/475°F/Gas 9.

5. Prick several holes in the buns with a skewer or cocktail stick. Bake them for 30–35 minutes, until golden brown. Switch off the oven, but leave the buns in it for a further 5 minutes.

6. Transfer the buns to a wire cooling rack and sprinkle them with cold water.

Above: Flat rye buns
Below: Pitta bread

Spelt crispbread

Easy

Crispbread is quick and easy to make and absolutely delicious to eat. Do not bake it until it goes brown – it should dry rather than bake. A fan-assisted oven is ideal for baking crispbread.

Makes 16 slices
120 ml/4 fl oz milk
50 g/2 oz butter, plus extra
*   for greasing*
250 g/9 oz wholemeal spelt flour,
*   plus extra for dusting*
5 ml/1 teaspoon sea salt

Approximately per slice:
330 kj/79 kcal
2 g protein
3 g fat
10 g carbohydrate

● Approximate preparation
   time: 1 hour 25 minutes,
   including standing and
   cooking

1. Heat the milk with the butter in a small saucepan over a low heat until the butter has melted. Sift together the flour and salt into a large bowl.

2. Pour the warm milk over the flour mixture and stir gently into a fairly firm, but smooth dough. Form the dough into a ball, cover and set aside for about 30 minutes. Grease a baking sheet. Preheat the oven to 180°C/350°F/Gas 4 (fan-assisted oven: 160°C/325°F).

3. Cut the dough ball in half and roll out one half on a lightly floured surface to a 20 cm/8 inch square. Cut the rolled-out dough into 8 rectangles and arrange them on the baking sheet. Prick each with a fork several times. Repeat with the remaining dough.

4. Bake the crispbread for about 20–25 minutes, until crisp and golden brown. Transfer the crispbread to a wire rack to cool.

Tip

You can also make this crispbread with wholemeal rye flour. However, the rye dough is a little harder to work with.

Sweet wheatgerm crispbread

Exquisite

Home-baking enables you to make delicious treats that you cannot buy in the shops, such as this sweet crispbread made with healthy wheatgerm. It tastes wonderful with a cup of tea or coffee and, spread with butter and honey or jam, makes a delightful alternative to cake. Home-made crispbread tastes superbly fresh and crunchy. You can store it in a container with a tight-fitting lid, but don't keep it for more than a fortnight or it will lose its freshness.

Makes 16 slices
200 g/7 oz plain white flour
75 ml/5 tablespoons wheatgerm or
*   60 ml/4 tablespoons oat bran*
50 g/2 oz brown sugar
5 ml/1 teaspoon baking powder
50 g/2 oz butter, softened, plus
*   extra for greasing*
105 ml/7 tablespoons milk
60–75 ml/4–5 tablespoons wheat
*   germ or oat bran, for dusting*

Approximately per slice:
390 kj/93 kcal
6 g protein
2 g fat
15 g carbohydrate

● Approximate preparation time: 1³/₄ hours, including standing and cooking

---

1. Sift the flour into a large bowl and stir in the wheat germ, sugar and baking powder. Cut the butter into small pieces, then rub it into the flour mixture with your fingertips or using an electric mixer until fully incorporated.

2. Make a well in the centre of the flour mixture and pour the milk into it. Gradually work the ingredients together to form a fairly firm, but smooth dough. Form into a ball, cover and set aside for about 30 minutes.

3. Grease a baking sheet. Preheat the oven to 180°C/350°F/Gas 4 (fan-assisted oven: 160°C/325°F). Sprinkle the work surface with wheat germ or oat bran. Cut the dough in half and roll out one half to a 20 cm/8 inch square. Cut the rolled-out dough into 8 rectangles. Place them on the baking sheet and prick with a fork. Repeat with the remaining dough.

4. Bake the crispbread for about 30–35 minutes, until golden brown. Switch off the oven, but leave the crispbread in it for a further 5 minutes. Then transfer to a wire rack to cool.

Soya rolls

Easy

Makes 16 rolls
300 g/11 oz strong white flour,
 plus extra for dusting
50 g/2 oz soya flour
15 g/1 1/2 oz vanilla sugar
30 g/1 1/4 oz fresh yeast
15 ml/1 tablespoon clear honey
250 ml/8 fl oz lukewarm water
5 ml/1 teaspoon salt
butter, for greasing

Approximately per roll:
390 kj/93 kcal
4 g protein
0 g fat
17 g carbohydrate

● Approximate preparation
 time: 1 hour 40 minutes,
 including rising and cooking

1. Sift the flours into a large bowl, stir in the sugar and make a well in the centre. Crumble the yeast into the well and add the honey and water. Stir to mix the yeast, honey and a little of the flour into a thin paste. Cover and set aside in a warm place for about 15 minutes.

2. Gradually knead in the rest of the flour and the salt. Form the dough into a ball, cover and set aside for about 15 minutes. Grease a baking sheet.

3. Knead the dough until smooth and elastic, then roll out on a lightly floured surface to a 40 cm/16 inch long roll. Divide the roll into 16 equal pieces. Turn each piece over in the flour, then shape into a 10 cm/4 inch long roll. Place 8 rolls close together on the baking sheet to make 2 x 25 cm/10 inch long loaves. Cover and set aside in a warm place for about 10 minutes, until the bulk of the dough has increased by one-third.

4. Meanwhile, spray the floor and sides of the oven with water. Preheat it to 240°C/475°F/Gas 9.

5. Brush the loaves with a little water and bake for 30–35 minutes, until golden brown. Switch off the oven, but leave the loaves in it for a further 5 minutes.

6. Transfer the loaves to a wire rack. Sprinkle or brush them all over with cold water. When cool, break them into individual rolls.

Oat bran rolls

Easy

Makes 16 rolls
300 g/11 oz strong white flour, plus
 extra for dusting
50 g/2 oz oat bran
15 g/1 1/2 oz vanilla sugar
30 g/1 1/4 oz fresh yeast
15 ml/1 tablespoon clear honey
250 ml/8 fl oz lukewarm milk
pinch of salt
butter, for greasing
15 ml/1 tablespoon milk,
 for brushing

Approximately per roll:
380 kj/90 kcal
4 g protein
1 g fat
16 g carbohydrate

● Approximate preparation
 time: 1 hour 40 minutes,
 including rising and cooking

1. Sift the flour into a large bowl, stir in the oat bran and sugar and make a well in the centre. Crumble the yeast into the well and add the honey and milk. Mix the yeast, honey and a little of the flour mixture to a thin paste. Cover and set aside in a warm place for about 15 minutes.

2. Gradually knead in the rest of the flour and the salt. Form the dough into a ball, cover and set aside for about 15 minutes. Grease a baking sheet.

3. Knead the dough until smooth and elastic. Roll out on a floured surface to a 40 cm/16 inch long roll. Divide the roll into 16 pieces. Turn each piece in the flour, then shape into a 10 cm/4 inch long roll. Place 8 rolls close together on the baking sheet to make 2 x 25 cm/10 inch long loaves. Cover and set aside in a warm place for about 10 minutes, until the bulk of the dough has increased by one-third. Brush the tops with the milk.

4. Meanwhile, spray the floor and sides of the oven with water. Preheat it to 240°C/475°F/Gas 9.

5. Bake the loaves for about 30–35 minutes, until golden brown. Switch off the oven, but leave the loaves in it for a further 5 minutes.

6. Transfer the loaves wire rack. Sprinkle or brush them all over with cold water. When cool, break the loaves into individual rolls.

Above: Soya rolls
Below: Oat bran rolls

Focaccia

For guests • Italian speciality

Makes 1 large loaf
600 g/1 lb 5 oz strong white flour
40 g/1¹/2 oz fresh yeast
10 ml/2 teaspoons sugar
400 ml/14 fl oz lukewarm water
60 ml/4 tablespoons olive oil
15 ml/1 tablespoon salt
100 g/3³/4 oz butter, plus extra
    for greasing
15 ml/1 tablespoon coarse salt

Approximately per portion:
790 kj/190 kcal
4 g protein
9 g fat
22 g carbohydrate

● Approximate preparation
  time: 1 hour 50 minutes,
  including rising and cooking

---

1. Sift the flour into a large bowl and make a well in the centre. Crumble the yeast into the well and sprinkle the sugar over it. Pour in the water and mix the yeast, sugar and a little of the flour to a thin paste. Cover and set aside in a warm place for 15 minutes.

2. Gradually knead in the rest of the flour, the oil and salt to make a firm dough. Form the dough into a ball, cover and set aside for about 15 minutes. Grease a baking sheet.

3. Knead the dough until smooth and elastic. Place on the baking sheet and spread it out flat with a pastry slice or spatula. Push up the edges a little to make a rim. Cover and set aside for a further 15 minutes, until the bulk of the dough has increased by one-third.

4. Meanwhile, spray the floor and sides of the oven with water. Preheat it to 230°C/450°F/Gas 8.

5. Prick the loaf all over with a two-pronged fork. Dot the butter over the top and sprinkle evenly with the coarse salt. Bake the focaccia for 30–35 minutes, until golden brown. Switch off the oven, but leave the loaf in it for a further 10 minutes.

6. Remove the focaccia from the oven, sprinkle the top with water and set aside on the baking sheet for 10 minutes. Carefully slide the loaf on to a wire rack. Serve warm or cold.

Variations
Focaccia with tomatoes
Instead of topping the loaf with butter and salt, sprinkle it with a mixture of 250 g/9 oz tomato purée, 60 ml/4 tablespoons olive oil, 5 ml/1 teaspoon dried *herbes de provence*, 2.5 ml/¹/2 teaspoon salt and 2.5 ml/½ teaspoon freshly ground black pepper. Prick the top all over with a fork. Immediately after removing the loaf from the oven, sprinkle at least 75 ml/ 5 tablespoons olive oil over it.

Focaccia with olives
Omit the butter and sea salt topping. Instead, roughly chop about 20 stoned black olives and sprinkle them over the dough. Sprinkle 150 ml/¹/4 pint olive oil over the dough and season to taste with freshly ground black pepper. Prick the loaf all over with a fork. Immediately after removing the loaf from the oven, sprinkle at least another 75 ml/5 tablespoons olive oil over it.

Potato focaccia
Peel and thinly slice 500 g/1 ¹/4 lb floury potatoes and blanch them for about 1 minute in at least 1 litre/1³/4 pints gently boiling water. Omit the butter and salt topping and arrange the potato slices over the dough. Sprinkle 150 ml/¹/4 pint olive oil over them, together with 5 ml/1 teaspoon dried rosemary, 2.5 ml/ ¹/2 teaspoon salt and about 1.5 ml/¹/4 teaspoon freshly ground black pepper. Immediately after removing the loaf from the oven, sprinkle a further 75 ml/ 5 tablespoons olive oil over it.

Focaccia Quattro Stagione
Use a quarter of the above toppings, spreading each over one quarter of the dough.

Focaccia, an Italian rustic bread, makes a delicious between-meals snack.

Bavarian beer breadsticks

Easy

Makes 12
200 g/7 oz stoneground white flour,
    plus extra for dusting
50 g/2 oz rye flour
20 g/³/4 oz fresh yeast
5 ml/1 teaspoon sugar
120 ml/4 fl oz lukewarm water
20 g/³/4 oz lard
2.5 ml/¹/2 teaspoon salt
5 ml/1 teaspoon baking powder
butter, for greasing
1 small egg, lightly beaten
10 ml/2 teaspoons caraway seeds
5 ml/1 teaspoon coarse salt

Approximately per portion:
370 kj/88 kcal
2 g protein
2 g fat
16 g carbohydrate
● Approximate preparation time: 1¹/2 hours, including rising and cooking

1. Sift the flours into a large bowl and make a well in the centre. Crumble the yeast into the well and sprinkle the sugar over it. Pour in the water and mix the yeast, sugar and a little of the flour mixture to a thin paste. Cover and set aside in a warm place for about 15 minutes.

2. Gradually knead in the rest of the flour mixture, the lard and 2.5 ml/½ teaspoon salt, adding the baking powder towards the end with the last of the dry flour mixture. Form the dough into a ball, cover and set aside for 15 minutes. Grease a baking sheet.

3. Knead the dough until smooth and elastic. Roll out on a lightly floured surface, then divide into 12 pieces and shape into 20 cm/ 8 inch sticks. Brush the breadsticks with beaten egg and sprinkle with the caraway seeds and coarse salt. Place them on the baking sheet, spacing them well apart and set aside for a further 15 minutes.

4. Meanwhile, spray the floor and sides of the oven with water. Preheat it to 240°C/475°F/Gas 9.

5. Bake the breadsticks for about 25 minutes, until crisp and golden brown. Switch off the oven, but leave the breadsticks in it for a further 5 minutes. Transfer to a wire rack to cool.

Grissini

Italian speciality

Makes 16
250 g/9 oz stoneground white flour
20 g/³/4 oz fresh yeast
5 ml/1 teaspoon sugar
120 ml/4 fl oz lukewarm water
50 g/2 oz butter, softened, plus
    extra for greasing
5 ml/1 teaspoon salt
5 ml/1 teaspoon baking powder
about 30 ml/2 tablespoons
    poppy seeds

Approximately per portion:
340 kj/81 kcal
2 g protein
3 g fat
12 g carbohydrate
● Approximate preparation time: 1¹/2 hours, including rising and cooking

1. Sift the flour into a large bowl and make a well in the centre. Crumble the yeast into the well and sprinkle the sugar over it. Pour in the water and mix the yeast, sugar and a little of the flour to a thin paste. Cover and set aside in a warm place for about 15 minutes.

2. Knead in the rest of the flour, the butter and salt, adding the baking powder towards the end with the last of the dry flour. Form the dough into a ball, cover and set aside for 15 minutes. Grease a baking sheet.

3. Meanwhile, spray the floor and sides of the oven with water. Preheat it to 240°C/475°F/Gas 9.

4. Knead the dough until smooth and elastic. Sprinkle half the poppy seeds on to a work surface and place the dough ball on top. Roll out and divide the dough into 16 pieces. Form each piece into a 30 cm/12 inch long stick. Coat them in poppy seeds (not too many or the dough slides about). Place the sticks on the baking sheet, spacing them well apart. Do not let the dough rise any more.

5. Bake the grissini for about 25 minutes, until crisp and golden brown. Switch of the oven, but leave the grissini in it for a further 5 minutes. Transfer to a wire rack and sprinkle with the remaining poppy seeds.

Right: Grissini
Left: Bavarian beer breadsticks

Curd cheese rolls

Quick • Easy

Makes 16
300 g/11 oz plain white flour
15 ml/1 tablespoon baking powder
5 ml/1 teaspoon salt
5 ml/1 teaspoon sugar
250 g/9 oz curd cheese
50 g/2 oz butter, softened, plus
    extra for greasing
10 ml/2 teaspoons poppy or
    caraway seeds

Approximately per portion:
410 kj/98 kcal
4 g protein
3 g fat
14 g carbohydrate

● Approximate preparation
   time: 50 minutes, including
   cooking time

1. Sift the flour into a large bowl and stir in the baking powder, salt and sugar. Add the curd cheese and the butter and knead quickly to make a firm, smooth dough. If the ingredients do not blend into the dough completely – when the cheese is too dry – add a little water. Form the dough into a ball.

2. Grease a baking sheet. Preheat the oven to 190°C/375°F/Gas 5 (fan-assisted oven: 180°C/350°F).

3. Divide the dough into 4 pieces and then divide each piece into 4 more. Form each piece into a ball. Arrange them on the baking sheet and flatten slightly to about 2 cm/³/4 inch thick. Sprinkle with water and scatter the seeds over them, gently pressing the seeds in.

4. Bake the rolls for about 25–30 minutes, until golden brown. Switch off the oven, but leave the rolls in it for a further 5 minutes,

5. Transfer the rolls to a wire rack and sprinkle them with cold water. Leave to cool.

Muffins

Quick

Makes 12
250 g/9 oz plain white flour, plus
    extra for dusting
10 ml/2 teaspoons baking powder
5 ml/1 teaspoon salt
5 ml/1 teaspoon sugar
pinch of ground black pepper
pinch of freshly grated nutmeg
150 ml/¹/4 pint Greek-style yogurt
105 ml/7 tablespoons double cream
105 ml/7 tablespoons curd cheese
icing sugar, for dusting (optional)

Approximately per portion:
470 kj/112 kcal
4 g protein
3 g fat
17 g carbohydrate

● Approximate preparation
   time: 50 minutes, including
   cooking time

1. Sift together the flour, baking powder, salt, sugar, black pepper and grated nutmeg into a large bowl and make a well in the centre. Add the Greek-style yogurt, cream and curd cheese to the well and gradually knead in the dry ingredients to form a soft, smooth dough. Shape the dough into a ball.

2. Sprinkle 12 paper cake cases with a little flour and arrange them on a baking sheet. Preheat the oven to 190°C/375°F/Gas 5 (fan-assisted oven: 180°C/350°F).

3. Using a wet knife, divide the dough into 4 pieces, then divide each piece into 3 more, wetting the knife blade again if necessary. With wet hands form each piece into a ball and place them in the prepared paper cases.

4. Bake the muffins for about 25–30 minutes, until golden brown. Switch off the oven, but leave the muffins in it for a further 5 minutes.

5. Transfer the muffins to a wire rack. Spray or brush the tops with cold water. When cold, dust them with a little flour or icing sugar, if liked.

Above: Curd cheese rolls
Below: Muffins

Classic white loaf

Economical

Makes 1 x 1 kg/2¼ lb loaf

750 g/1 lb 10 oz strong white flour
40 g/1½ oz fresh yeast
15 ml/1 tablespoon sugar
500 ml/18 fl oz lukewarm water
15 ml/1 tablespoon salt
butter, for greasing

**Approximately per
50 g/2 oz slice:**
740 kj/180 kcal
6 g protein
1 g fat
37 g carbohydrate

● Approximate preparation
time: 2½ hours, including
rising and cooking

---

1. Sift the flour into a large bowl
and make a well in the centre.
Crumble the yeast into the well
and sprinkle the sugar over it. Pour
in the water and mix the yeast,
sugar and a little of the flour into a
thin paste. Cover the bowl and set
aside for about 15 minutes in a
warm place.

2. Gradually knead in the rest of
the flour together with the salt
until fully incorporated. Form the
dough into a ball, cover and set
aside for about 15 minutes. Grease
a 1 kg/2¼ lb loaf tin.

3. Knead the dough until smooth
and elastic. Roughly shape it into a
loaf, place it in the prepared tin
and flatten gently with a spatula.
Cover and set aside in a warm
place for a further 15 minutes,
until the bulk of the dough has
increased by one-third.

4. Spray the floor and sides of the
oven with water. Preheat the oven
to 200°C/400°F/Gas 6.

5. Bake the bread for about
1¼ hours, until it is golden brown
on top. Turn off the oven, but
leave the bread in it for a further
10 minutes.

6. Remove the bread from the
oven and turn out on to a wire
rack. Spray or brush cold water all
over the loaf and leave to cool.

Variations

To make a milk loaf, use:
750 g/1 lb 10 oz strong white flour
40 g/1½ oz fresh yeast
30 ml/2 tablespoons sugar
500 ml/18 fl oz lukewarm milk
5 ml/1 teaspoon salt
115 g/4 oz sultanas.

Make the dough as above and
bake for 1 hour 10 minutes.

To make a cheese loaf, use:
750 g/1 lb 10 oz strong,
   white flour
40 g/1½ oz fresh yeast
30 ml/2 tablespoons sugar
250 ml/8 fl oz lukewarm water
500 g/1¼ lb curd cheese
115 g/4 oz currants or sultanas
50 g/2 oz melted butter.

Make the dough as above and
bake for 1¼ hours.

Tip

Home-made white bread tastes
best when freshly baked, but it
can be stored for 2–3 days.
Serve it with sausage or cheese.
Serve milk or cheese bread
with jam, honey, marmalade or
other sweet spreads.

*Delicious white bread, such as the Milk
bread shown here, as well as toast bread,
is quite easy to bake at home*

Tuscan white bread

Rather time-consuming

This virtually salt-free bread is especially delicious topped with Italian salami or Parma ham.

Makes 1 x 600 g/1 lb 5 oz loaf

400 g/14 oz strong white flour, plus
    extra for dusting
20 g/³/4 oz fresh yeast
2.5 ml/¹/2 teaspoon sugar
250 ml/8 fl oz lukewarm water
pinch of salt
butter, for greasing

**Approximately per
50 g/2 oz slice:**
490 kj/120 kcal
4 g protein
0 g fat
24 g carbohydrate

● Approximate preparation
   time: 2¹/2 hours, including
   rising and cooking

---

1. Sift the flour into a large bowl and make a well in the centre. Crumble the yeast into the well and sprinkle the sugar over it. Pour in the water and mix the yeast, sugar and a little of the flour to a thin paste. Cover and set aside for about 20 minutes in a warm place.

2. Gradually knead in the rest of the flour and the salt. Form the dough into a ball, cover and set aside for about 30 minutes. Grease a baking sheet.

3. Knead the dough until smooth and elastic. Dust the work surface with flour and flour your hands.

Shape the dough into a ball, roll it in the flour and place on the baking sheet. Flatten to form a 20 cm/8 inch round. Cover and set aside in a warm place for a further 20 minutes, until the bulk of the dough has increased by one-third.

4. Meanwhile, spray the floor and sides of the cold oven with water. Preheat it to 240°C/475°F/Gas 9.

5. Bake the loaf for about 1 hour, until golden brown. Turn off the oven, but leave the loaf in it for a further 15 minutes.

6. Transfer the loaf to a wire rack. Spray or brush cold water all over it and leave to cool.

Baguette

Rather time-consuming

Makes 2 x 275 g/10 oz loaves

400 g/14 oz strong white flour, plus
    extra for dusting
20 g/³/4 oz fresh yeast
2.5 ml/¹/2 teaspoon sugar
250 ml/8 fl oz lukewarm water
10 ml/2 teaspoons salt
butter, for greasing

Approximately per loaf:
2,900 kj/690 kcal
22 g protein
2 g fat
150 g carbohydrate

● Approximate preparation
   time: 2¹/2 hours, including
   rising and cooking

---

1. Sift the flour into a large bowl and make a well in the centre.

Crumble the yeast into the well and sprinkle the sugar over it. Pour in the water and mix the yeast, sugar and a little of the flour to a thin paste. Cover and set aside for about 20 minutes in a warm place.

2. Gradually knead in the rest of the flour and the salt. Form the dough into a ball, cover and set aside for about 30 minutes. Grease a baking sheet.

3. Knead the dough until smooth and elastic. Lightly dust the work surface with a little flour and flour your hands. Divide the dough into 2 pieces and form each piece into a roll about 40 cm/16 inches long. Place them on the baking sheet, spaced well apart, and flatten each roll to 5–6 cm/2–2¹/2 inches wide.

4. Cover the loaves and set aside in a warm place for a further 20 minutes, until the bulk of the dough has increased by one-third.

5. Meanwhile, spray the floor and sides of the cold oven with water. Preheat it to 240°C/475°F/Gas 9.

6. Bake the loaves for about 45 minutes, until they are golden brown. Turn off the oven, but leave the loaves in it for a further 15 minutes.

7. Transfer the loaves to a wire rack. Spray or brush cold water all over them and leave to cool.

Above: Tuscan white bread
Below: Baguette

Spelt toasting loaf

Easy

It is no problem to bake your own toasting bread. It is best cooked in a fan-assisted oven and using an ovenproof glass dish, so that it does not become too crusty, making it better for toasting.

Makes 1 x 675 g/1 1/2 lb loaf

200 g/7 oz spelt flour
115 g/4 oz strong white flour
115 g/4 oz plain white flour
25 g/1 oz fresh yeast
250 ml/8 fl oz lukewarm water
30 ml/2 tablespoons clear honey
50 g/2 oz butter, softened, plus
*   extra for greasing*
1 egg yolk
10 ml/2 teaspoons salt

Approximately per 50 g/2 oz slice:
620 kj/150 kcal
4 g protein
4 g fat
24 g carbohydrate

● Approximate preparation time: 2 hours, including rising and cooking

---

1. Sift all three types of flour into a large bowl and make a well in the centre. Crumble the yeast into the well and add the water and honey. Mix the yeast, water, honey and a little of the mixed flours to a thin paste. Cover the bowl and set aside for about 15 minutes in a warm place.

2. Gradually knead in the rest of the flour and the butter, egg yolk and salt. Form the dough into a ball, cover and set aside for about 15 minutes. Grease a 675 g/1 1/2 lb loaf tin with a little butter.

3. Knead the dough until smooth and elastic. Shape the dough into a loaf, place it in the prepared tin and flatten it with a spatula. Cover and set aside in a warm place for a further 15 minutes, until the bulk of the dough has increased by about one-third.

4. Meanwhile spray the floor and sides of the cold oven with water. Preheat it to 190°C/375°F/Gas 5 (fan-assisted oven: 180°C/350°F). Bake the loaf for about 45 minutes, until golden brown. Turn off the oven, but leave the loaf in it for 10 minutes, then transfer to a wire rack to cool.

Crispy toast bread

Exquisite

Makes 1 x 675g/1½ lb loaf

115 g/4 oz millet
25 g/1 oz butter, plus extra
  for greasing
30 ml/2 tablespoons poppy seeds
300 g/11 oz strong white flour
25 g/1 oz fresh yeast
30 ml/2 tablespoons soft
  brown sugar
105 ml/7 tablespoons
  lukewarm water
1 egg yolk
120 ml/4 fl oz single cream
5 ml/1 teaspoon salt

**Approximately per
50 g/2 oz slice:**
710 kj/170 kcal
4 g protein
6 g fat
24 g carbohydrate

● Approximate preparation
time: 2 hours, including rising
and cooking

1. Put the millet into a sieve, pour 1 litre/1¾ pints boiling water over it and drain. Melt the butter in a frying pan and fry the poppy seeds and millet, stirring, for 2–3 minutes. Remove from the heat. Sift the flour into a bowl and make a well in the centre. Crumble the yeast into the well, add the sugar and water and mix with a little of the flour to a thin paste.

2. Cover the bowl and set aside for about 15 minutes in a warm place. Then gradually knead in the remaining flour, together with the egg yolk, cream, salt and the millet mixture. Form the dough into a ball, cover and set aside for a further 15 minutes.

3. Grease a 675 g/1½ lb loaf tin. Knead the dough thoroughly again and shape into a loaf. Place the dough in the prepared tin and flatten it with a spatula. Cover and set aside for about 15 minutes in a warm place, until the bulk of the dough has increased by one-third.

Tip

You can also wipe over the floor and sides of the oven with a well-dampened cloth to provide a steamy atmosphere for cooking the bread. Then, preheat the oven as usual.

4. Meanwhile, spray the floor and sides of the cold oven with water. Preheat it to 190°C/375°F/Gas 5 (fan-assisted oven: 180°C/350°F). Bake the loaf for about 45 minutes until golden brown. Turn off the oven, but leave the loaf in it for a further 10 minutes, then transfer to a wire rack to cool.

27

Golden toast loaf

Easy

Makes 1 x 800 g/1³/₄ lb loaf

500 g/1¹/₄ lb strong white flour
40 g/1¹/₂ oz fresh yeast
30 ml/2 tablespoons sugar
300 ml/1¹/₂ pint lukewarm water
50 g/2 oz butter, diced, plus extra
*   for greasing*
2 egg yolks
2 teaspoons salt

**Approximately per
40 g/1¹/₂ oz slice:**
480 kj/114 kcal
3 g protein
3 g fat
20 g carbohydrate

● Approximate preparation
  time: 2 hours, including rising
  and cooking

1. Sift the flour into a large bowl
and make a well in the centre.
Crumble the yeast into the well
and sprinkle the sugar over it. Pour
in the water and mix the yeast,
sugar and a little of the flour to a
thin paste. Cover and set aside in a
warm place for 15 minutes.

2. Gradually knead in the rest of
the flour and the butter, egg yolks
and salt. Form the dough into a
ball, cover and set aside for about
15 minutes. Grease an 800 g/
1³/₄ lb loaf tin.

3. Knead the dough until smooth
and elastic and shape into a loaf.
Place it in the tin and press it flat.
Cover and set aside in a warm
place for a further 15 minutes,
until the bulk of the dough has
increased by about one-third.

4. Meanwhile, spray the floor and
sides of the cold oven with water.
Preheat it to 190°C/375°F/Gas 5
(fan-assisted oven: 180°C/350°F).

5. Bake the loaf for 50 minutes,
until golden brown. Turn off the
oven, but leave the loaf in it for a
further 10 minutes. Remove from
the oven and turn out on to a wire
rack. Sprinkle or brush cold water
all over it. Do not cut the bread
until the next day.

Rye toast bread

Easy

Makes 1 x 900 g/2 lb loaf

300 g/11 oz strong white flour
200 g/7 oz rye flour
40 g/1¹/₂ oz fresh yeast
15 ml/1 tablespoon sugar
15 ml/1 tablespoon black treacle
250 ml/8 fl oz lukewarm buttermilk
120 ml/4 fl oz crème fraîche
10 ml/2 teaspoons salt
butter, for greasing

**Approximately per
40 g/1¹/₂ oz slice:**
430 kj/100 kcal
3 g protein
3 g fat
17 g carbohydrate

● Approximate preparation
  time: 2 hours, including rising
  and cooking

1. Sift the flours into a large bowl
and make a well in the centre.
Crumble the yeast into the well
and pour the sugar and treacle
over it. Add the buttermilk and
mix the yeast, sugar, treacle and a
little of the flour to a thin paste.
Cover and set aside in a warm
place for 15 minutes.

2. Gradually knead in the rest of
the flour and the crème fraîche
and salt. Form the dough into a
ball, cover and set aside for about
15 minutes. Grease a 900 g/2 lb
loaf tin.

3. Knead the dough until smooth
and elastic and shape into a loaf.
Place it in the tin and press it flat.
Cover and set aside in a warm
place for a further 15 minutes,
until the bulk of the dough has
increased by about one-third.

4. Meanwhile, spray the floor and
sides of the cold oven with water.
Preheat it to 190°C/375°F/Gas 5
(fan-assisted oven: 180°C/350°F).

5. Bake the loaf for about 1 hour,
until golden brown. Turn off the
oven, but leave the loaf in it for a
further 10 minutes.

6. Remove the loaf from the oven
and turn out on to a cooling rack.
Sprinkle or brush cold water all
over it and leave to cool. Do not
cut the bread until the next day.

Above: Golden toast loaf
Below: Rye toast bread

Farmhouse bread

Easy

Makes 1 x 675 g/1 1/2 lb loaf

300 ml/1/2 pint water
2 tablespoons lard
2 tablespoons vinegar
300 g/11 oz strong white flour, plus extra for dusting
200 g/7 oz rye flour
40 g/1 1/2 oz fresh yeast
5 ml/1 teaspoon sugar
10 ml/2 teaspoons salt
butter, for greasing

Approximately per 50 g/2 oz slice:
590 kj/140 kcal
4 g protein
3 g fat
26 g carbohydrate

● Approximate preparation time: 2³/4 hours, including rising and cooking

1. Heat the water with the lard and vinegar in a small saucepan over a low heat, until the lard has melted. Remove the pan from the heat and set aside to cool slightly.

2. Sift the flours together into a bowl and make a well in the centre. Crumble the yeast into the well and add the sugar and lukewarm vinegar mixture. Mix the yeast, sugar, vinegar mixture and a little of the flour to a thin paste. Cover and set aside in a warm place for about 15 minutes.

3. Gradually knead in the rest of the flour and the salt. Form the dough into a ball, cover and set aside for about 20 minutes. Grease a baking sheet.

4. Knead the dough until smooth and elastic. Lightly dust the work surface with flour. Shape the dough into a ball and roll it in the flour. Place on the baking sheet and flatten slightly with your hands to a 20 cm/8 inch round. Cover and set aside in a warm place for about 15 minutes, until the bulk of the dough has increased by one-third.

5. Meanwhile, spray the floor and sides of the cold oven with water. Preheat it to 220°C/400°F/Gas 6.

6. Bake the bread for 1 hour, until golden brown. Turn off the oven, but leave the loaf in it a further 10–15 minutes.

7. Transfer the loaf to a wire rack and sprinkle or brush cold water all over it. Leave to cool.

Swiss country bread

Economical

Light brown bread is extremely popular in Switzerland and Austria, but you don't have to be Swiss to enjoy this delicious loaf.
Makes 1 x 675 g/1 1/2 lb

250 g/9 oz strong white flour, plus extra for dusting
250 g/9 oz Granary flour
40 g/1 1/2 oz fresh yeast
5 ml/1 teaspoon sugar
300 ml/1/2 pint lukewarm water
10 ml/2 teaspoons salt
butter, for greasing

Approximately per 50 g/2 oz slice:
520 kj/120 kcal
1 g protein
4 g fat
12 g carbohydrate

● Approximate preparation time: 2³/4 hours, including rising and cooking

1. Sift the flours into a large bowl and make a well in the centre. Crumble the yeast into the well and sprinkle the sugar over it. Pour in the water and mix the yeast, sugar and a little of the flour to a thin paste. Cover and set aside in a warm place for about 15 minutes.

2. Gradually knead in the rest of the flour and the salt. Form the dough into a ball, cover and set aside for about 20 minutes. Grease a baking sheet.

3. Knead the dough until smooth and elastic. Dust the work surface with flour. Form the dough into a ball and roll it in the flour. Place on the baking sheet and flatten to a 20 cm/8 inch round. Cover and set aside in a warm place for about 15 minutes, until the bulk of the dough has increased by one-third.

4. Meanwhile, spray the floor and sides of the cold oven with water. Preheat it to 220°C/400°F/Gas 6.

5. Bake for 1 hour, until golden. Turn off the oven, but leave the loaf in it for 10–15 minutes. Transfer to a wire rack and sprinkle or brush cold water all over it.

Above: Farmhouse bread
Below: Swiss country bread

Bavarian sourdough bread

Must be started well in advance

This spicy bread is the perfect edible gift. It is also excellent to serve when you have guests. Crisp, freshly-baked bread goes with every dish and ensures that there will be plenty to satisfy even the heartiest appetite.

Makes 1 x 1.2 kg/2½ lb loaf

200 g/7 oz strong white flour
15 ml/1 tablespoon clear honey
500 ml/18 fl oz lukewarm water
200 g/7 oz Granary flour
200 g/7 oz rye flour
200 g/7 oz wholemeal flour
15–30 ml/1–2 tablespoons Bavarian
   spice mixture (equal quantities of
   caraway, coriander and fennel
   seeds), plus extra for sprinkling
6.5 ml/1¼ teaspoons salt
butter, for greasing

For the sourdough starter:
75 g/3 oz wholemeal or rye flour
75 g/3 oz strong white flour
50 g/2 oz sugar
250 ml/8 fl oz milk

Approximately per 50 g/2 oz slice
460 kj/110 kcal
4 g protein
0 g fat
23 g carbohydrate

● Approximate preparation time: 2½ hours, including rising and cooking, plus 5 days for the sourdough starter

---

1. First, make the sourdough starter 5 days before baking the bread. Sift the two types of flour into an earthenware crock and add the sugar and milk. Beat well until thoroughly combined and the mixture is smooth.

2. Cover and set aside at room temperature for 5 days, until the mixture is frothy and has a strong, sour smell.

3. To make the bread, sift the strong white flour into a large mixing bowl and make a well in the centre. Add the sourdough starter, honey and water to the well and mix. Cover and set aside in a warm place for 15 minutes.

4. Add the Granary flour, rye flour, wholemeal flour, Bavarian spice mixture, to taste, and salt to the bowl and mix gently together. Gradually knead them into the dough. Form the dough into a ball, cover and set aside for 15 minutes. Grease a baking sheet.

5. Knead the dough until smooth and elastic. With wet or floured hands form the dough into a ball and place it on the baking sheet. Flatten slightly with your hands to a 25 cm/10 inch round. Spray lightly with water and sprinkle Bavarian spice mixture evenly over it. Gently press the seeds on to the bread.

6. Cover the loaf and set aside in a warm place for about 15 minutes, until the bulk of the dough has increased by one-third.

7. Meanwhile, spray the floor and sides of the cold oven with water. Preheat to 200°C/400°F/Gas 6.

8. Bake the loaf for about 1¼ hours, until crisp and brown. Turn off the oven, but leave the loaf in it for a further 10 minutes.

9. Transfer the loaf to a wire rack and sprinkle or brush with cold water all over it. Leave to cool.

Tip

The only raising agent in this loaf is the sourdough starter. It is affected by the surrounding temperature and humidity, so it can take longer than 5 days before it is ready. If you are in any doubt about whether it will work, you can add a paste made by mixing 15 g/½ oz fresh yeast, 1.5 ml/¼ teaspoon sugar and 30 ml/2 tablespoons lukewarm water with the sourdough starter in step 2.

Bavarian sourdough bread makes a very special present.

Double-baked bread

Easy

Wholemeal bread has a deliciously chewy texture and, as the bran and germ of the whole wheat grain are present in the flour, it is particularly nutritious.

Makes 1 x 1 kg/2¹/₄ lb loaf

650 g/1 lb 7 oz wholemeal flour, plus extra for dusting
40 g/1¹/₂ oz fresh yeast
15 ml/1 tablespoon sugar
500 ml/18 fl oz lukewarm water
15 ml/1 tablespoon sea salt
butter, for greasing

Approximately per 50 g/2 oz slice:
470 kj/112 kcal
4 g protein
1 g fat
23 g carbohydrate

● Approximate preparation time: 3 hours, including rising and cooking

---

1. Sift the flour into a large bowl and tip in any bran remaining in the sieve. Make a well in the centre. Crumble the yeast into the well and sprinkle the sugar over it. Pour in the water and mix the yeast, sugar and a little of the flour to a thin paste.

2. Cover the bowl with a cloth and set aside in a warm place for about 15 minutes, until the yeast mixture becomes frothy.

3. Gradually knead in the rest of the flour and the salt until thoroughly incorporated. Form the dough into a ball, cover and set aside for about 30 minutes.

4. Knead the dough until smooth and elastic. Grease a 1 kg/2¹/₄ lb loaf tin with butter, sprinkle in about 15 ml/1 tablespoon flour and shake to coat. Put the dough into the tin and flatten the top with a spatula. Sprinkle a little flour over the top.

5. Cover and set aside in a warm place for 15 minutes, until the bulk of the dough has increased by about one-third.

6. Spray the floor and sides of the cold oven with water. Preheat the oven to 200°C/400°F/Gas 6.

Tip

You can use this double-baking method for any bread made from a yeast-dough, especially if you like your bread crusty. If after baking the bread does not look crusty enough, spray it with water as usual, and put it back into the oven at 200°C/400°F/Gas 6 for a further 10–20 minutes. Then spray or brush it all over with water again. Leave it to cool on a cooling rack.

Test whether the loaf is cooked by tapping the base with your knuckles. If it sounds hollow, the bread is ready.

7. Bake the bread for about 1 hour, until golden brown. Turn off the oven, but leave the loaf in it for a further 10 minutes.

8. Turn the loaf out on to a wire rack and spray or brush cold water all over it. Return the loaf, without the tin, to the oven and bake again at 200°C/400°F/ Gas 6 for about 20–25 minutes, until crusty and golden brown. Transfer the loaf to a wire rack and spray or brush it with water again. Leave to cool.

Six-grain bread

Rather time-consuming

Bread containing lots of different kinds of grain not only tastes superb, but it is also very healthy.

Makes 1 x 1 kg/2¹/4 lb loaf

50 g/2 oz coarse soya flour
50 g/2 oz sunflower seeds
50 g/2 oz oat groats
500 ml/18 fl oz water
50 g/2 oz linseed
500 g/1¹/4 lb strong white flour,
*   plus extra for dusting*
115 g/4 oz rye flour
40 g/1¹/2 oz fresh yeast
15 ml/1 tablespoon clear honey
15 ml/1 tablespoon sea salt
butter, for greasing

Approximately per 50 g/2 oz slice:
600 kj/140 kcal
6 g protein
3 g fat
24 g carbohydrate

● Approximate preparation time: 2³/4 hours, including rising and cooking

---

1. Dry-fry the soya flour, sunflower seeds and oat groats in a large, heavy-based frying pan over a low heat, stirring constantly, until they begin to give off a fragrant aroma. Carefully pour in the water, remove the pan from the heat and stir in the linseed. Set aside to cool to lukewarm.

2. Sift the strong white and rye flours into a large mixing bowl and make a well in the centre. Crumble the yeast into the well and add the clear honey and the lukewarm mixture from the frying pan. Mix the yeast, honey, warm seed mixture and a little of the flour, to make a thin paste. Cover and set aside in a warm place for 15 minutes.

3. Gradually knead in the rest of the flour flour and the salt. Form the dough into a ball, cover and set aside for about 15 minutes. Grease a baking sheet and dust with a little flour.

4. Knead the dough again until smooth and elastic. With wet hands, form the dough into a ball and place it on the baking sheet. Flatten slightly with wet hands to a 25 cm/10 inch round.

5. Cover and set aside in a warm place for 15 minutes, until the bulk of the dough has increased by one-third.

6. Meanwhile, spray the floor and sides of the cold oven with water. Preheat it to 200°C/400F/Gas 6.

7. Bake the loaf for about 50 minutes, until golden brown. Turn off the oven, but leave the loaf in it for a further 10 minutes.

8. Transfer the loaf to a wire rack and spray or brush cold water all over it. Leave to cool.

Variations

Depending on the grains and seed used, this recipe can be adapted in a wide variety of ways – even to suit allergies and special dietary requirements. Instead of soya flour you could use buckwheat, or even rye, wheat, barley or spelt seeds. You could replace the sunflower seeds with pumpkin seeds or nuts, such as coarsely chopped hazelnuts or walnuts. Substitute coarse oat flakes, millet or quinoa for the oat groats.

Six-grain bread, made with a mixture of grains and seeds, is utterly delicious.

Sunflower seed bread

Rather time-consuming

Makes 1 x 1 kg/2^1/4 lb loaf

115 g/4 oz sunflower seeds
50 g/2 oz linseed
50 g/2 oz oat groats
50 g/2 oz millet
50 g/2 oz buckwheat
500 ml/18 fl oz boiling water
250 g/9 oz plain white flour
250 g/9 oz wholemeal flour
40 g/1½ oz fresh yeast
10 ml/2 teaspoons clear honey
10–15 ml/2–3 teaspoons sea salt
butter, for greasing

**Approximately per
50 g/2 oz slice:**

600 kj/140 kcal
6 g protein
4 g fat
21 g carbohydrate

● Approximate preparation
time: 3 hours, including
rising and cooking

---

1. Dry-fry the sunflower seeds
until they give off their aroma. Set
aside. Put the linseed, oats, millet
and buckwheat in a bowl and pour
in the boiling water. Stir well, cover
and set aside for about 1 hour.

2. Sift the flour into a large bowl
and make a well in the centre.
Crumble the yeast into the well.
Add the honey, linseed and soaking
water. Mix with a little flour to
make a paste. Cover and set aside
in a warm place for 15 minutes.

3. Gradually knead in the rest of
the flour and the salt. Form the

dough into a ball, cover and leave
in a warm place for 15 minutes.
Grease a 1 kg/2^1/4 lb loaf tin.

4. Knead the dough until smooth
and elastic. Sprinkle the sunflower
seeds on it and knead in. Form the
dough into a loaf, place it in the tin
and flatten slightly with a spatula.

5. Spray the floor and sides of the
cold oven with water. Preheat the
oven to 200°C/400°F/Gas 6.

6. Bake the loaf for 1 hour, until
golden. Turn off the oven, but
leave the loaf in it for 10 minutes.
Turn out the loaf on to a wire rack
and spray or brush cold water all
over it. If wished, double bake the
loaf (see page 35).

Linseed bread

Easy

Makes 1 x 1 kg/2^1/4 lb loaf

115 g/4 oz linseed
500 ml/18 fl oz boiling water
250 g/9 oz strong white flour
250 g/9 oz wholemeal flour
40 g/1½ oz fresh yeast
10 ml/2 teaspoons clear honey
10–15 ml/2–3 teaspoons sea salt
butter, for greasing

**Approximately per
50 g/2 oz slice:**

450 kj/108 kcal
4 g protein
2 g fat
18 g carbohydrate

● Approximate preparation
time: 3 hours, including
rising and cooking

---

1. Put the linseed in a bowl, pour
in the boiling water and stir well.
Cover and set aside for 1 hour.

2. Sift the flour into a large bowl
and make a well in centre.
Crumble the yeast into the well
and add the honey. Pour in the
linseed and the soaking water. Mix
the honey and linseed mixture
with a little of the flour, to form a
paste. Cover and set aside in a
warm place for 15 minutes.

3. Gradually knead in the rest of
the flour and the salt. Form the
dough into a ball, cover and set
aside in a warm place for
15 minutes. Grease a 1 kg/2^1/4 lb
loaf tin.

4. Knead the dough until smooth
and elastic. Shape the dough into a
loaf, place it in the tin and flatten
slightly with a spatula. Slash the top
diagonally with a knife.

5. Spray the floor and sides of the
cold oven with water. Preheat the
oven to 200°C/400°F/Gas 6.

6. Bake the loaf for about 1 hour,
until golden brown. Turn off the
oven, but leave the loaf in it for a
further 10 minutes. Turn out the
loaf on to a cooling rack and spray
or brush cold water all over it. If
wished, double-bake the loaf (see
page 35).

Above: Linseed bread
Below: Sunflower seed bread

Spelt bread

Exquisite • Easy

Spelt is beginning to enjoy a revival of popularity because few other grains makes such light bread that tastes so scrumptious and is so easy to digest. The high albumen content makes it excellent for kneading and baking. You can obtain spelt flour from some organic or health-food shops.

Makes 1 x 1 kg/2¼ lb loaf

500 g/1¼ lb wholemeal spelt flour
250 g/9 oz white spelt flour
40 g/1½ oz fresh yeast
15 ml/1 tablespoon clear honey
500 ml/18 fl oz lukewarm water
15 ml/1 tablespoon sea salt
butter, for greasing

**Approximately per
50 g/2 oz slice:**
530 kj/127 kcal
5 g protein
1 g fat
25 g carbohydrate

● Approximate preparation
time: 2½ hours, including
rising time and cooking time

1. Sift the flours into a large bowl and make a well in the centre. Crumble the yeast into the well and add the honey. Pour in the water and mix the yeast, honey and a little of the flour to a thin paste. Cover the bowl and set aside in a warm place for about 15 minutes.

2. Gradually knead in the rest of the flour mixture and the salt. Form the dough into a ball, cover and set aside in a warm place for about 15 minutes. Grease a 1 kg/2¼ lb loaf tin.

3. Knead the dough until smooth and elastic. Shape the dough into a loaf, place it in the tin and flatten slightly with a spatula. Cover and set aside in a warm place for about 15 minutes, until the bulk of the dough has increased by one-third.

4. Meanwhile, spray the floor and sides of the cold oven with water. Preheat it to 220°C/425°F/Gas 7.

5. Bake the bread for about 1 hour, until golden brown. Turn off the oven, but leave the loaf in it for a further 10 minutes.

6. Turn out the loaf on a wire rack and spray or brush cold water all over it.

7. If the loaf is still very pale in colour or even a little soft, return it, without its tin, to the oven and bake at 200°C/400°F/Gas 6 for about 15 minutes, until it turns golden brown.

8. Transfer to a wire rack and spray or brush it with water. Leave to cool.

Variations
You can vary spelt bread according to taste or what is available in the shops. For example, use 500 g/1¼ lb spelt flour and 250 g/9 oz wholemeal spelt flour, or replace half the spelt flour with 250 g/9 oz strong white flour. Or just use 750 g/1 lb 10 oz wholemeal spelt flour. The largest quantity of flour should always be spelt flour, or the bread will lose its characteristic aroma and consistency.

Bake a deliciously light and soft loaf with spelt flour. It not only tastes wonderful, but is also very easy to digest.

Graham bread

Rather time-consuming

Named after the revolutionary American nutritionist, Sylvester Graham, this bread is made exclusively from wholemeal flour. As long ago as the early nineteenth century, Graham led a crusade against what he saw as his country's bad eating habits, advocating a diet high in bran and much lower in red meat and hot spices. The pre-soaked wholemeal flour certainly makes the bread particularly light and digestible and it smells simply wonderful while it is cooking.

Makes 1 x 950 g/2 lb 2 oz loaf

500 g/1 1/4 lb wholemeal flour
10 ml/2 teaspoons salt
375 ml/13 fl oz boiling water
20 g/3/4 oz fresh yeast
10 ml/2 teaspoons brown sugar
50 ml/2 fl oz lukewarm milk
115 g/4 oz strong white flour
butter, for greasing

Approximately per 50 g/2 oz slice:
370 kj/88 kcal
3 g protein
1 g fat
17 g carbohydrate

● Approximate preparation time: 4 hours, including rising and cooking

---

1. Sift half the wholemeal flour into a large bowl and tip in any bran remaining in the sieve. Stir in the salt. Pour in the water and mix well. Set the bowl aside for at least 30 minutes.

2. Make a well in the centre of the mixture, crumble in the yeast and sprinkle the sugar over it. Pour in the milk, add half the strong white flour and mix all the ingredients in the well. Cover the bowl and set aside in a warm place for about 30 minutes.

3. Gradually knead in all the rest of the flour. Form the dough into a ball, cover and set aside in a warm place for a further 30 minutes. Grease 950 g/2 lb 2 oz loaf tin.

4. Knead the dough until smooth and elastic. Shape the dough into a loaf, place it in the tin and flatten it slightly with a spatula. Cover and set aside in a warm place for about 30 minutes, until the bulk of the dough has increased by one-third.

5. Meanwhile, spray the floor and sides of the cold oven with water. Preheat the oven to 190°C/375°F/Gas 5 (fan-assisted oven: 180°C/350°F).

6. Bake the loaf for 1 1/4 hours, until golden brown. Turn off the oven, but leave the loaf in it for a further 10 minutes.

7. Turn the loaf out on to a wire rack and spray or brush cold water all over it.

8. If the loaf is still very pale in colour, return it, without the tin, to the oven and bake again at 200°C/400°F/Gas 6 for a further 15 minutes, until it turns golden brown.

9. Transfer the loaf to a wire rack and spray or brush it all over with cold water again, then leave to cool completely.

Variation
Wheat-bran bread
In step 1, add 115 g/4 oz wheat bran and increase the quantity of boiling water to 500 ml/18 fl oz.

Tip

Graham bread has a very dense texture which means that it stores extremely well.

To make Graham bread, the wholemeal flour is pre-soaked to make it extra digestible.

Army bread

Easy

Makes 1 x 750 g/1 lb 10 oz loaf

250 g/9 oz rye flour, plus extra
*   for dusting*
250 g/9 oz wholemeal flour
40 g/1 1/2 oz fresh yeast
15 ml/1 tablespoon black treacle
300 ml/1/2 pint lukewarm water
10 ml/2 teaspoons salt
10 ml/2 teaspoons caraway seeds
butter, for greasing

**Approximately per
50 g/2 oz slice:**
460 kj/110 kcal
4 g protein
1 g fat
23 g carbohydrate

● Approximate preparation
time: 3 hours, including
rising and cooking

---

1. Sift the flours into a large bowl and tip in any bran remaining in the sieve. Make a well in the centre. Crumble the yeast into the well and pour the treacle and water over it. Mix the yeast, treacle, water and a little of the flour to a thin paste. Cover and set aside in a warm place for about 15 minutes.

2. Gradually knead in the rest of the flour, the salt and caraway seeds. Form the dough into a ball, cover and set aside in a warm place for about 1 hour. Grease a baking sheet.

3. Knead the dough until smooth and elastic. Dust a work surface with rye flour and flour your hands. Roll the dough into a 20 cm/8 inch long sausage and place on the baking sheet. Cover and set aside in a warm place for 20 minutes, until the bulk of the dough has increased by one-third.

4. Meanwhile, spray the floor and sides of the cold oven with water. Preheat it to 220°C/425°F/Gas 7.

5. Bake the loaf for about 1 hour, until golden brown. Turn off the oven, but leave the loaf in it for a further 10 minutes. Transfer the loaf to a wire rack and spray or brush cold water all over it. Leave to cool.

Mixed rye bread

Easy

Makes 1 x 750 g/1 lb 10 oz loaf

350 g/12 oz rye flour, plus extra
*   for dusting*
150 g/5 oz strong white flour
40 g/1 1/2 oz fresh yeast
15 ml/1 tablespoon black treacle
300 ml/1/2 pint lukewarm water
10 ml/2 teaspoons salt
5 ml/1 teaspoon caraway seeds
butter, for greasing

**Approximately per
50 g/2 oz slice:**
470 kj/112 kcal
3 g protein
0g fat
25 g carbohydrate

● Approximate preparation
time: 3 hours, including
rising and cooking time

---

1. Sift the flours into a large bowl and tip in any bran remaining in the sieve. Make a well in the centre. Crumble the yeast into the well and pour the treacle and water over it. Mix the yeast, treacle, water and a little of the flour to a thin paste. Cover and set aside in a warm place for 15 minutes.

2. Gradually knead in the rest of the flour, the salt and caraway seeds. Form the dough into a ball, cover and set aside in a warm place for about 1 hour. Grease a baking sheet.

3. Knead the dough until smooth and elastic. Dust a work surface with rye flour and flour your hands. Roll the dough into a 20 cm/8 inch sausage and place on the baking sheet. Cover and set aside in a warm place for about 20 minutes, until the bulk of the dough has increased by one-third.

4. Meanwhile, spray the floor and sides of the cold oven with water. Preheat it to 220°C/425°F/Gas 7.

5. Bake the loaf for about 1 hour, until golden brown. Turn off the oven, but leave the loaf in it for a further 10 minutes.

6. Transfer the loaf to a cooling rack and spray or brush cold water all over it. Leave to cool.

Tip

Mixed rye bread will keep for about a week.

Above: Army bread
Below: Mixed rye bread

Traditional rye bread

Rather time-consuming

The dough ferments naturally, so this is a very easy bread to make – it almost makes itself. All it requires is a small, warm corner of the kitchen (at least 23°C/73°F) for 1–3 days. After fermentation, the dough is so damp and sticky, that thorough mixing with a strong wooden spoon or in a food processor is enough. Using a wider tin than usual, such as a well-greased roasting tin, helps the loaf to cook evenly.

Makes 1 x 1.5 kg/3½ lb loaf

115 g/4 oz clear honey
750 ml/1¼ pints lukewarm water
1 kg/2¼ lb wholemeal rye flour,
  freshly ground if possible
15 ml/1 tablespoon sea salt
15–30 ml/1–2 tablespoons
  caraway seeds
butter, for greasing

**Approximately per
50 g/2 oz slice:**
450 kj/118 kcal
4 g protein
1 g fat
21 g carbohydrate

● Approximate preparation
time: 5¼ hours, including
rising and cooking, plus
1–3 days fermenting time

---

1. Mix together the honey and water and stir until the honey has dissolved. Sift the flour into a large bowl (preferably stainless steel) and make a well in the centre. Pour the honey mixture into the well and mix in about one-fifth of the flour to form a thin paste.

2. Cover the bowl with a tea towel and set aside in a warm place for 1–3 days, until the mixture becomes frothy, gently stirring the mixture on the second day to incorporate a little more of the flour.

3. Gradually knead in the rest of the flour and the salt and caraway seeds. Cover and set aside for about 10 minutes, then briefly stir the mixture again. Form the dough into a ball.

4. Grease a large tin. Place the dough in the prepared tin and flatten slightly with a spatula. Cover and set aside in a warm place for a further 1–3 hours, until the bulk of the dough has almost doubled. (If the room temperature is too low, this can take longer. Do not bake the loaf before the dough has visibly increased in bulk.)

5. Spray the floor and sides of the cold oven with water. Preheat the oven to 190°C/375°F/Gas 5.

6. Bake the loaf for about 1½ hours, until golden brown. Turn off the oven, but leave the loaf in it for a further 15 minutes.

7. Remove the tin from the oven. Spray or brush the top of the loaf with cold water and set aside to cool in the tin for 1 hour. Then transfer the loaf to a cooling rack to cool completely.

Tip

Another easy technique for making bread that does not involve yeast is to use bicarbonate of soda as the raising agent. This is also a very quick method, as you do not have to wait several days for the starter or to set the dough aside to rise. For Easy wholemeal bread, sift 450 g/1 lb wholemeal flour, 115 g/4 oz plain white flour, 5 ml/1 teaspoon salt, 6.5 ml/1¼ teaspoons bicarbonate of soda and 5 ml/1 teaspoon cream of tartar into a large bowl. Tip any bran remaining in the sieve into the bowl. Gradually stir in 300 ml/½ pint milk and 30 ml/2 tablespoons black treacle to form a soft dough. Knead briefly on a lightly floured surface, then shape into a 15 cm/6 inch round and place on a greased baking sheet. Cut a cross in the top and bake in a preheated oven, 220°C/425°F/Gas 7, for 40–45 minutes. Transfer the loaf to a wire rack to cool slightly, then serve warm with plenty of butter.

This Traditional rye bread does take a little time, but waiting for the natural fermentation of the dough is well worth while.

Corn bread

Exquisite • Quick

This American speciality is an essential accompaniment to chilli con carne. It is fairly bland, so it also goes very well with other hot, Tex-Mex dishes. Make sure all the ingredients are at the same temperature before you start, so that the mixture does not curdle.

Makes 1 x 600 g/1 lb 5 oz loaf

150 g/5 oz fine cornmeal
50 g/2 oz cornflour
50 g/2 oz plain white flour
45 ml/1 tablespoon baking powder
15 ml/1 teaspoon salt
15 ml/1 teaspoon dried basil
130 g/4¹/₂ oz butter, softened, plus
*   extra for greasing*
130 g/4¹/₂ oz curd cheese
3 eggs

**Approximately per
65 g/2¹/₂ oz slice:**
900 kj/210 kcal
6 g protein
13 g fat
20 g carbohydrate

● Approximate preparation
time: 1 hour 10 minutes,
including cooking

1. Preheat the oven to 190°C/ 375°F/Gas 5 (fan assisted oven: 180°C/350°F). Sift together the cornmeal, cornflour, plain flour, baking powder and salt into a large bowl and stir in the basil. Gradually beat in the butter, curd cheese and the eggs to form a creamy batter.

2. Grease a 600 g/1 lb 5 oz loaf tin. Spoon the batter into the prepared tin and smooth the surface with a spatula.

3. Bake the loaf for 40–45 minutes until golden brown, or until a thin skewer or cocktail stick inserted into the centre of the loaf comes out clean. (If necessary, bake the loaf for a further 5–10 minutes.)

4. Turn off the oven, but leave the loaf in it for a further 10 minutes. Remove the tin from the oven and spray or brush the top of the loaf with water. Leave to cool in the tin.

Buckwheat bread

Quick

As corn bread goes with Tex-Mex dishes, so buckwheat bread goes well with all highly spiced European dishes. Thick slices of bread can be frozen and then thawed in the toaster, so you always have a quick accompaniment to hand.

Makes 1 x 600 g/1 lb 5 oz loaf

130 g/4 1/2 oz buckwheat flour
130 g/4 1/2 oz plain white flour
15 ml/1 tablespoon baking powder
5 ml/1 teaspoon salt
130 g/4 1/2 oz butter, softened,
  plus extra for greasing
130 g/4 1/2 oz curd cheese
3 eggs

**Approximately per
65 g/2 1/2 oz slice:**
910 kj/220 kcal
2 g protein
13 g fat
20 g carbohydrate

● Approximate preparation
time: 1 1/4 hours, including
cooking time

1. Preheat the oven to 190°C/ 375°F/Gas 5 (fan-assisted oven: 180°C/350°F). Sift the buckwheat flour, plain flour, baking powder and salt into a large mixing bowl. Using an electric mixer, gradually beat in the butter, curd cheese and eggs to form a creamy batter.

2. Grease 600 g/1 lb 5 oz loaf tin. Spoon the batter into the prepared tin and smooth the surface with a spatula.

3. Bake the loaf for 55 minutes, until golden brown and a fine skewer or cocktail stick inserted into the centre comes out clean. (If necessary, bake the bread for a further 5–10 minutes.)

4. Turn off the oven, but leave the loaf in it for a further 10 minutes. Remove the tin from the oven and spray or brush the top of the loaf with cold water. Leave to cool completely in the tin.

Poppy seed loaf

Easy

Makes 1 x 1 kg/2¼ lb loaf

650 g/1 lb 7 oz strong white flour,
   plus extra for dusting
40 g/1½ oz fresh yeast
5 ml/1 teaspoon sugar
500 ml/18 fl oz lukewarm buttermilk
60 ml/4 tablespoons poppy seeds
5 ml/1 teaspoon fennel seeds
5 ml/1 tsp aniseed
50 g/2 oz butter, softened
15 ml/1 tablespoon salt
butter, for greasing

**Approximately per
50 g/2 oz slice:**
590 kj/140 kcal
5 g protein
3 g fat
25 g carbohydrate

● Approximate preparation
   time: 3 hours, including
   rising and cooking

1. Sift the flour into a large bowl
and make a well in the centre.
Crumble the yeast into the well
and sprinkle the sugar over it. Add
the buttermilk and mix the yeast,
sugar and a little of the flour into a
paste. Cover and set aside for
about 15 minutes.

2. Dry-fry the seeds in a heavy-
based frying pan over a low heat.

3. Knead the remaining flour, the
butter, toasted seeds and salt into
the dough. Form it into a ball,
cover and set aside for 25 minutes.

4. Knead the dough well. Grease a
baking sheet and dust a 25 cm/
10 inch rattan basket with flour.
Form the dough into a ball, place it
in the basket and flatten slightly.
Cover and set aside in a warm
place for 20 minutes, until the bulk
of the dough has increased by
about one-third. Then carefully tip
it on to the baking sheet.

5. Spray the floor and sides of the
cold oven with water. Preheat the
oven to 220°C/425°F/Gas 7.

6. Bake the loaf for 45 minutes,
then reduce the temperature to
190°C/375°F/Gas 5 and bake for a
further 20–30 minutes. Turn off
the oven, but leave the loaf in it for
a further 15 minutes. Transfer the
loaf to a wire rack and spray or
brush cold water all over it. Leave
to cool completely.

Spicy white bread

Exquisite

Makes 1 x 1.2 kg/2½ lb loaf

650 g/1 lb 7 oz strong white flour,
   plus extra for dusting
40 g/1½ oz fresh yeast
5 ml/1 teaspoon sugar
250 ml/8 fl oz water
150 ml/¼ pint Greek-style yogurt
50 g/2 oz butter, softened, plus
   extra for greasing
115 g/4 oz Emmental cheese, diced
25 g/1 oz pistachio nuts,
   coarsely chopped
115 g/4 oz Parma ham, diced
1 fresh red chilli, seeded and
   finely chopped
5 ml/1 teaspoon cumin seeds
15 ml/1 tablespoon salt

**Approximately per
50 g/2 oz slice:**
1,200 kj/290 kcal
10 g protein
10 g fat
37 g carbohydrate

● Approximate preparation
   time: 3 hours, including
   rising and cooking

1. Sift the flour into a large bowl
and make a well in the centre.
Crumble the yeast into the well
and sprinkle the sugar over it. Add
the water and yogurt and mix to a
thin paste with a little of the flour.
Cover and set aside in a warm
place for about 15 minutes.

2. Knead in the remaining flour,
the butter, cheese, pistachios, ham,
chilli, cumin and salt. Form the
dough into a ball, cover and set
aside for about 25 minutes.

3. Knead the dough well. Grease a
baking sheet and dust a 25 cm/
10 inch rattan basket with flour.
Form the dough into a ball, place it
in the basket and flatten slightly.
Cover and set aside in a warm
place for 20 minutes. Carefully tip
it on to the baking sheet.

4. Spray the floor and sides of the
cold oven with water. Preheat it to
220°C/425°F/Gas 7. Bake the loaf
for 45 minutes, then reduce the
temperature to 190°C/375°F/
Gas 5 and bake for 20–30 minutes.
Turn off the oven, but leave the
loaf in it for a further 15 minutes.
Transfer the loaf to a cooling rack
and spray or brush cold water.

Above: Poppy seed loaf
Below: Spicy white bread

Camembert bread

Exquisite • Easy

With a slightly over-ripe Camembert cheese and a little flour, you can easily conjure up a delicious and unusual loaf that your guests will love.

Makes 1 x 900 g/2 lb loaf

250 g/9 oz strong white flour
250 g/9 oz wholemeal flour
40 g/1¹/₂ oz fresh yeast
5 ml/1 teaspoon sugar
250 ml/8 fl oz lukewarm water
130 g/4¹/₂ oz over-ripe Camembert
* cheese, diced*
130 g/4¹/₂ oz curd cheese
5 ml/1 teaspoon salt
5 ml/1 teaspoon sweet paprika
butter, for greasing

**Approximately per
50 g/2 oz slice:**
530 kj/130 kcal
6 g protein
3 g fat
20 g carbohydrate

● Approximate preparation
  time: 2¹/₄ hours, including
  rising and cooking

I. Sift the flours into a large bowl and make a well in the centre. Crumble the yeast into the well and sprinkle the sugar over it. Pour in the water and mix the yeast, sugar and a little of the flour to a thin paste. Cover with a tea towel and set aside in a warm place for about 15 minutes.

2. Gradually knead in the rest of the flour, the Camembert, curd cheese, salt and paprika. Form the dough into a ball, cover and set aside for about 15 minutes. Grease a rectangular, ovenproof glass dish about 28 cm/11 inches long.

3. Knead the dough until smooth and elastic. Shape the dough into a loaf, place it in the prepared dish and flatten slightly with a spatula. Cover and set aside in a warm place for about 15 minutes, until the bulk of the dough has increased by one-third.

4. Meanwhile, spray the floor and sides of the cold oven with water. Preheat it to 200°C/400°F/Gas 6.

5. Bake the loaf for 1¹/₄ hours, until golden brown. Turn off the oven, but leave the loaf in it for a further 15 minutes.

6. Turn out the loaf on to a cooling rack and spray or brush cold water all over it. If it is still very pale in colour or even a little soft, return it, without the dish, to the oven and bake for a further 15 minutes at 200°C/ 400°F/Gas 6 until it turns golden brown.

7. Transfer to a cooling rack and spray or brush it with water again. Leave to cool completely.

Variation
You can also bake rolls using the same dough. Divide the dough into 12–16 equal-size pieces and form them into balls with wet hands. Place them in a greased cake tin and flatten slightly. Spray the tops with water, and if desired, sprinkle with caraway, poppy or pumpkin seeds, gently pressing them in. Bake the rolls in a preheated oven at 200°C/400°F/Gas 6 for about 30–40 minutes, until golden brown. Turn out on to a wire rack to cool.

Tip

Camembert is ripe to serve as a table cheese when it has a supple rind and the cheese bulges gently when pressed, but does not run. It deteriorates very quickly – usually within two to three days. Over-ripe cheese that has become runny is perfect for this bread, but do not use it if it has become hard or smells bitter.

Would you have thought that there was actually a Camembert cheese in this delicious loaf? Try it for yourself.

Emmental cake bread

For guests

Of course, you can also bake this bread in a loaf tin or any other kind of tin, but if you use a springform cake tin, it looks especially attractive. If you chill the butter in the freezer for about 1 hour beforehand, the loaf acquires holes – just like the cheese. It tastes delicious either still slightly warm or cold and goes particularly well with a glass of wine or sherry.

Makes 1 x 25 cm/10 inch round loaf

500 g/1 ¼ lb strong white flour
10 ml/2 teaspoons salt
1.5 ml/¼ teaspoon freshly ground
 black pepper
250 g/9 oz Emmental
 cheese, grated
40 g/1 ½ oz fresh yeast
10 ml/2 teaspoons sugar
250 ml/8 fl oz lukewarm water
250 g/9 oz curd cheese
2 eggs
50 g/2 oz chilled butter, finely diced,
 plus extra for greasing

Approximately per slice:
860 kj/200 kcal
10 g protein
8 g fat
24 g carbohydrate

● Approximate preparation time: 3 hours, including rising and cooking

---

1. Sift the flour into a large bowl and stir in the salt, pepper and grated cheese. Make a well in the centre, crumble in the yeast and sprinkle the sugar over it. Pour in the water and the yeast, sugar and a little of the flour mixture to a thin paste. Cover and set aside in a warm place for about 15 minutes.

2. Gradually knead in the rest of the flour, the curd cheese and eggs. Form the dough into a ball, cover and set aside for about 25 minutes. Grease a 25 cm/10 inch springform cake tin.

3. Knead the dough until smooth and elastic. Finally, knead in the butter, distributing the pieces evenly. Form the dough into a ball, place it in the prepared tin and flatten slightly with a spatula. Cover with a clean tea towel and set aside in a warm place for a further 25 minutes, until the bulk of the dough has increased by about one-third.

4. Meanwhile, spray the floor and sides of the cold oven with water. Preheat it to 200°C/400°F/Gas 6.

5. Bake the loaf for about 1 hour, until golden. Turn off the oven, but leave the loaf in it for a further 15 minutes.

6. Remove the tin from the oven and spray or brush the top of the loaf with cold water. Unfasten the tin and leave the bread to cool. Transfer to a cooling rack to cool completely.

Tip

Emmental is a semi-hard cheese with a mellow flavour and is ideal for cooking – although it is an excellent table cheese as well. When buying, avoid cheese that has a lot of holes or that shows any sign of cracking. The best Emmental still comes from Switzerland, where the cheese originated.

Emmental cake bread is a good accompaniment to a dinner party menu. Your guests will love it.

Onion bread

Exquisite

Makes 1 x 1 kg/2¼ lb loaf

120 ml/4 fl oz sunflower oil
400 g/14 oz onions, diced
115 g/4 oz wholemeal flour
115 g/4 oz rye flour
500 g/1¼ lb strong white flour
2.5 ml/½ teaspoon freshly ground
  black pepper
40 g/1½ oz fresh yeast
5 ml/1 teaspoon sugar
500 ml/18 fl oz lukewarm water
15 ml/1 tablespoon salt
butter, for greasing
30 ml/2 tablespoons caraway seeds

**Approximately per
50 g/2 oz slice:**
430 kj/100 kcal
2 g protein
52 g carbohydrate

● Approximate preparation
  time: 3 hours, including
  rising and cooking

---

1. Heat the oil in a frying pan and fry the onions for 8–10 minutes, until golden. Remove the pan from the heat and set aside to cool.

2. Sift the flours and pepper into a large bowl and make a well in the centre. Crumble the yeast into the well and sprinkle the sugar over it. Pour in the water and with a little of the flour to a thin paste. Cover and set aside in a warm place for about 15 minutes.

3. Gradually knead in the rest of the flour, the onions and salt. Form the dough into a ball, cover and set aside for 20 minutes..

4. Grease a baking sheet. Knead the dough again. Sprinkle the work surface with the seeds and roll the dough in them. Place on the baking sheet and flatten to a 25 cm/10 inch round. Cover and set aside for 25 minutes, until it has increased in bulk by one-third. Meanwhile, spray the floor and sides of the cold oven with water. Preheat it to 230°C/450°F/Gas 8.

5. Bake the loaf for 1 hour, until brown. Turn off the oven, but leave the loaf in it for 15 minutes. Then transfer to a wire rack and spray or brush with cold water.

Savoury bread

Rather time-consuming

Makes 1 x 1.2 kg/2½ lb loaf

250 g/9 oz smoked bacon, diced
400 g/14 oz onions, diced
115 g/4 oz wholemeal flour
115 g/4 oz rye flour
500 g/1¼ lb strong white flour
2.5 ml/1½ teaspoon freshly ground
  black pepper -
40 g/1½ oz fresh yeast
5 ml/1 teaspoon sugar
500 ml/18 fl oz lukewarm water
10 ml/2 teaspoons salt
butter, for greasing
30 ml/2 tablespoons caraway seeds

**Approximately per
50 g/2 oz slice:**
760 kj/182 kcal
5 g protein
9 g fat
22 g carbohydrate

● Approximate preparation
  time: 3¼ hours, including
  rising and cooking

---

1. Fry the bacon and onions in a frying pan over a medium heat until the bacon is crisp and the onions are golden. Remove the pan from the heat.

2. Sift the flours and pepper into a large bowl and make a well in the centre. Crumble the yeast into the well and sprinkle the sugar over it. Pour in the water and mix the yeast, sugar and a little of the flour to a thin paste. Cover and set aside in a warm place for about 15 minutes.

3. Gradually knead in the rest of the flour, the bacon and onions and the salt. Form the dough into a ball, cover and set aside for 20 minutes. Grease a baking sheet.

4. Knead the dough until smooth and elastic. Sprinkle the work surface with the caraway seeds. Form the dough into a ball and roll it in the seeds. Place on the baking sheet and flatten slightly with your hands to a 25 cm/10 inch round. Cover and set aside in a warm place for about 25 minutes, until it has increased in bulk by one-third.

5. Meanwhile, spray the floor and sides of the cold oven with water. Preheat it to 230°C/450°F/Gas 8.

6. Bake the loaf for about 1 hour, until crisp and brown. Turn off the oven, but leave the loaf in it for a further 15 minutes.

7. Transfer the loaf to a wire rack and spray or brush cold water all over it. Leave to cool.

Above: Onion bread
Below: Savoury bread

Aztec bread

Quite difficult

The secret of this loaf, which is golden brown and very aromatic, lies in an ingredient that is unusual in bread-making – chocolate. In fact, chocolate is used quite often in savoury dishes in Mexico. Plain chocolate is recommended here, but you could also use Mexican chocolate – if available – which is flavoured with cinnamon, almonds and vanilla. This loaf is a superb accompaniment to a wide variety of savoury dishes – hearty roast pork or chicken casserole, for example – and it is delicious with cheese and ham.

Makes 1 x 900 g/2 lb loaf

115 g/4 oz coarse rye flakes
120 ml/4 fl oz white wine vinegar
15 ml/1 tablespoon brown sugar
115 g/4 oz plain chocolate, broken
    into pieces
250 ml/8 fl oz lukewarm water
350 g/12 fl oz strong white flour
150 g/5 oz rye flour, plus extra
    for dusting
40 g/1 1/2 oz fresh yeast
120 ml/4 fl oz lukewarm milk
115g/4 oz single cream
15 ml/1 tablespoon salt
butter, for greasing

**Approximately per
50 g/2 oz slice:**
690 kj/160 kcal
4 g protein
4 g fat
28 g carbohydrate

● Approximate preparation
   time: 3 hours, including
   rising time cooking

---

1. Dry-fry the coarse rye flakes in a heavy-based frying pan over a low heat, stirring frequently, until they begin to give off a fragrant aroma. Transfer to a large bowl.

2. Add the white wine vinegar and sugar to the frying pan and stir over a low heat until the sugar has dissolved. Remove the pan from the heat and add the chocolate. Return the pan to a low heat and stir until the chocolate has melted. Gradually pour in the water, stirring constantly to make a smooth paste. Remove the pan from the heat and set aside to cool to lukewarm.

3. Sift the flours into the bowl with the rye flakes and make a well in the centre. Crumble the yeast into the well and pour in the lukewarm chocolate mixture and the milk. Mix with a little of the flour mixture to a thin paste. Cover and set aside in a warm place for 15 minutes.

4. Gradually knead in the rest of the flour, the cream and salt. Form the dough into a ball, cover and set aside for a further 15 minutes. Grease a baking sheet.

5. Knead the dough until smooth and elastic. Lightly dust a work surface with rye flour. Form the dough into a ball and roll it in the flour. Place on the prepared baking sheet and flatten slightly with your hands to a 25 cm/10 inch round.

6. Cover with a clean tea towel and set aside in a warm place for a further 15 minutes, until the bulk of the dough has increased by about one-third.

7. Meanwhile, spray the floor and sides of the cold oven with water. Preheat it to 220°C/425°F/Gas 7.

8. Bake the loaf for about 1 hour, until golden brown. Turn off the oven, but leave the loaf in it for a further 15 minutes.

9. Transfer the loaf to a wire rack and spray or brush cold water all over it. Leave to cool.

Aztec bread sounds mysterious – and the magic ingredient is an unguessable secret

Walnut bread

Easy

This aromatic bread tastes best when it is made with freshly shelled walnuts rather than the ready chopped ones available from supermarkets for cake making.

Makes 1 x 1 kg/2¼ lb loaf

*150 g/5 oz shelled walnuts,
    coarsely chopped
115 g/4 oz stoneground flour
350 g/12 oz strong white flour
150 g/5 oz rye flour, plus extra
    for dusting
40 g/1½ oz fresh yeast
15 ml/1 tablespoon brown sugar
250 ml/8 fl oz lukewarm water
120 ml/4 fl oz lukewarm milk
105 ml/7 tablespoons single cream
15 ml/1 tablespoon salt
butter, for greasing*

**Approximately per
50 g/2 oz slice:**
730 kj/174 kcal
5 g protein
7 g fat
24 g carbohydrate

● Approximate preparation
time: 2½ hours, including
rising and cooking

---

1. Dry-fry the walnuts in a heavy-based frying pan over a low heat, stirring frequently. Transfer the nuts to a large mixing bowl. Dry-fry the stoneground flour in the frying pan over a low heat, stirring constantly. Mix the toasted flour with the walnuts and leave to cool slightly.

2. Sift the white and rye flours into the mixing bowl and make a

well in the centre. Crumble the yeast into the well and sprinkle the sugar over it. Pour in the water and milk and mix the yeast, sugar and a little of the flour into a thin paste. Cover the bowl and set aside in a warm place for about 15 minutes.

3. Gradually knead in the rest of the flour, the cream and salt. Form the dough into a ball, cover and set aside for a further 15 minutes. Grease a baking sheet.

4. Knead the dough thoroughly again. Lightly dust a work surface with rye flour. Form the dough into a ball and roll it in the flour. Place on the prepared baking sheet and flatten slightly with your hands to a 25 cm/10 inch round.

5. Cover with a clean tea towel and set aside in a warm place for 15 minutes, until the bulk of the dough has increased by one-third.

6. Meanwhile, spray the floor and sides of the cold oven with water. Preheat it to 220°C/425°F/Gas 7.

7. Bake the loaf for about 1 hour, until golden brown. Turn off the oven, but leave the loaf in it for a further 15 minutes.

8. Transfer the loaf to a wire rack and spray or brush cold water all over it. Leave to cool.

Tip

If you want to make an even nuttier-tasting loaf, roll the dough in 115 g/4 oz coarsely chopped walnuts instead of rye flour.

Variation

For Walnut fruit bread, sift 350 g/12 oz plain white flour, 115 g/4 oz wholemeal flour and 5 ml/1 teaspoon salt into a large bowl and make a well in the centre. Crumble 15 g/½ oz fresh yeast into the well, add 30 ml/2 tablespoons sugar, 120 ml/4 fl oz lukewarm milk and 120 ml/4 fl oz lukewarm water and mix with a little of the flour mixture to a thin paste. Set aside for 15 minutes. Gradually knead in the rest of the flour and 150 ml/¼ pint soured cream. Turn out and knead until smooth and elastic. Form the dough into a ball, return to the clean bowl, cover and set aside for 1–1½ hours, until doubled in bulk. Knead the dough thoroughly again, then roll out into a rectangle. Sprinkle evenly with 50 g/2 oz finely chopped dried apricots, 50 g/2 oz sultanas and 75 g/3 oz chopped walnuts. Knead the dried fruit and nuts into the dough. Shape into a loaf and place in a greased 1 kg/2¼ lb loaf tin. Cover and set aside in a warm place for 30 minutes. Bake in a preheated oven, 220°C/425°F/Gas 7, for 40–45 minutes. Turn out on to a wire rack to cool.

This bread is something quite different – a walnut loaf with freshly chopped nuts. It tastes best eaten plain with butter.

INDEX

A
army bread 44
Aztec bread 58

B
bacon: savoury bread 56
baguette 24
baking: temperatures 5
    times 5
    tins and dishes 4
Bavarian beer breadsticks 18
Bavarian sourdough bread 32
breadsticks: Bavarian beer
    breadsticks 18
    grissini 18
brown breads 30–49
buckwheat bread 49

C
Camembert bread 52
Camembert rolls 52
cheese: Camembert bread 52
    Camembert rolls 52
    cheese loaf 22
    curd cheese rolls 20
    Emmental cake bread 54
    spicy white bread 50
classic white bread 22
corn bread 48
crispbread: spelt crispbread 12
    sweet wheatgerm
        crispbread 13
crispy toast bread 27
crusty rolls 8
curd cheese rolls 20

D
double-baked bread 34

E
easy wholemeal bread 46
Emmental cake bread 54
equipment 4

F
farmhouse bread 30
flat breads 8–21
flat rye buns 10
flours 6
focaccia 16
    potato 16
    quattro stagione 16
    with olives 16
    with tomatoes 16
fruit bread, walnut 60

G
golden toast loaf 28
Graham bread 42
grissini 18

L
linseed bread 38
liquid 5

M
milk bread 22
mistakes in bread-baking 5
mixed rye bread 44
muffins 20

O
oat bran rolls 14
onion bread 56
onions: onion bread 56
    savoury bread 56
oven 4
    temperature 5

P
pitta bread 10
poppy seed loaf 50
potato focaccia 16

R
rolls 8–21
rye bread: flat rye buns 10
    mixed rye bread 44
    rye toast bread 28
    traditional rye bread 46
rye toast bread 28

S

salt 7
seed rolls 8
seeds: linseed bread 38
   poppy seed loaf 50
   seed rolls 8
   spicy white bread 50
   sunflower seed bread 38
six-grain bread 36
sourdough 7
sourdough bread, Bavarian 32
soya rolls 14
speciality breads 50–61
spelt bread 40
   crispbread 12
   toasting loaf 24
spicy white bread 50
sunflower seed bread 38
sweet wheatgerm crispbread 13
Swiss country bread 30

T

toast bread: crispy toast bread 27
   golden toast loaf 28
traditional rye bread 46
Tuscan white bread 24

W

walnut bread 60
   fruit bread 60
wheat bran bread 22
white breads 22–29
wholemeal bread, easy 46

Y

yeast 5

Great Little Cook Books
Baking Bread

Published originally under the title *Brot backen* by Gräfe und Unzer Verlag GmbH, München

© 1993 by Gräfe und Unzer Verlag GmbH, München

English-language edition
© 2001 by Transedition Limited, Oxford, England

This edition published in 2001 by Advanced Marketing, Bicester, Oxfordshire

Translation:
Translate-A-Book, Oxford

Editing:
Linda Doeser Publishing Services, London

Typesetting:
Organ Graphic, Abingdon

10 9 8 7 6 5 4 3 2 1
Printed in Dubai

ISBN 1 901683 13 3

Important note

No grains should contain any dirt or weed seeds (particularly not the poisonous corn cockle). The same is true for ergot, which has become increasingly prevalent, especially in rye. It is easily recognized, blackish and the seed is usually greatly enlarged. Consumed in large quantities, ergot can be life-threatening. According to EC guidelines, grains may contain a maximum of 0.05 per cent ergot. That amounts to 3 seeds in 200 g/7 oz. It is very unlikely that any commercially produced flours will contain any undesirable residue. As well as many valuable components, bread baked with wholemeal flour may also contain unwanted substances, such as phytoacid. This binds proteins and mineral elements, such as iron, magnesium and zinc, so that they are less easily absorbed by the body. However, phytoacid content is decreased by the addition of yeast.

Note:

Quantities for all recipes are given in both metric and imperial measures and, if appropriate, in standard measuring spoons. They are not interchangeable, so readers should follow one set or the other.
5 ml = 1 teaspoon
15 ml = 1 tablespoon

Marey Kurz

comes from a German-Baltic family. When she was a young girl she often cooked for her parents and brothers and sisters and was interested in everything to do with eating and drinking. She has been cooking and baking for 25 years at home.

Odette Teubner

was trained by her father, the internationally renowned food photographer Christian Teubner. Today she works exclusively in the Teubner Studio for Food Photography. In her free time she is an enthusiastic photographer of children, using her own son as her model.

Dorothee Gödert

After completing her training, she worked first with still life and interior photography. Following a visit to Princeton in the United States, she began to specialize in food photography. She has worked with several well-known food photographers and has been with the Teubner Studio since 1988.